GOLDEN ADVICE OF PARENTS

Guidance from a father

Firdos Tarannum

ISBN 978-93-5610-103-6
© Firdos Tarannum 2021
Published in India 2021 by Pencil

A brand of

One Point Six Technologies Pvt. Ltd.
123, Building J2, Shram Seva Premises,
Wadala Truck Terminal, Wadala (E)
Mumbai 400037, Maharashtra, INDIA
E connect@thepencilapp.com
W www.thepencilapp.com

DISCLAIMER: *The opinions expressed in this book are those of the authors and do not purport to reflect the views of the Publisher.*

Author biography

Info about my father,

This is something what every kid admires of to talk about their father proudly,

This is the day to inform that this proud daughter's father name is MOHAMMED ABDUL MARUF he is from sindhanur of Raichur district in Karnataka state. he is a normal business man but also a member of islamic organization, helps people and motivational speaker(for children). Waking up and reading with cup of tea is a routine he does. Book reading and writing is second most loved thing for him after his family. He also writes poems with good teaching quality.

I want to say you have been the best in all your

fields, especially parenting and I love you dad for

sake of Allah.

Thank you,

Ammi(shahenaz khanam) and abbu(MA. Maruf)

For allowing us freely to choose our goals, thankyou for

hearing our problems and helping us to go through it.

Thankyou for guiding us all the way in life.

Thankyou for being the support, to fulfill our dreams..

Thankyou for you are the best and biggest blessing of

our life

CONTENTS

Foreword

This is the first ever edition of this book

It simply represents the beautiful relation between a daughter and a father which becomes extremely emotional when a daughter goes to an another home after her marriage

What she feels and miss about her father who shared a beautiful bond with her

Preface

When life becomes miserable or we feel

stuck at a certain point of life we miss our

only only wellwisher and supporter our

parents.

I started to miss them after my marriage,

every single advise of their became precious

only in their absence

We usually fail to express our love to our

Loved one, so I thought best would be to

express my love with beautiful words which

can be re-read.

Writing this so that the reader can get

benefit or feel helped during difficult times.

Acknowledgements

Guidance from a

FATHER

To her

DAUGHTER

Introduction

What more to say about the book

Words are not enough to describe the love of patents which keeps on increasing even after her daughter's marriage which just transfers from her to her children

It is an introduction of a daughter's journey after marriage where she misses her father and constantly reminds herself of his advice.

ADVICE PRIVATELY

It was evening time when my dad came to home and my mom asked me to arrange the dinner for him but I gave many excuses because I didn't wanted to do it, she watched me for a while then she arranged it for herself . Later at night she called me and asked me the reason I was ashamed to confess that I was lazy she then called me near and said, you are eating more than enough only because he earns yet you are lazy to serve him and she made me realise the importance of father.

Lesson

•Learn the importance before it's too late

•Realise each other's importance in life

•Serve your parents Because they served you with love

•Indeed , parents are beautiful way to Jannah

REALISE THE LOVE AROUND YOU

I had a very bad reaction of medicine unfortunately which got worst for every changed treatment , my mouth filled with ulcers with no food passage through mouth and at last my mouth swelled spitting atleast 3 handful of blood every night , I couldn't eat nor speak for a month but my mother understood my every action and finally after a month I showed symptoms of healing I started to eat like 6 month old from liquid to solid food to finally eating hard food , but the amazing thing that happened among all was my mother crying with joy upon hearing the word AMMI from my mouth, she was crying inconsolably. This reaction of her's made me to forget every pain.

Lesson

•There is no limit for mother's love

•Only difficulties make you realise the real worth

•You need only your loved one at rough phase

•Some problems require only patience

DO NOT COMPLAIN

I loved teaching and my father knew it and always helped me to reach as many places as I can to teach religion.

But I always complained of unavailable opportunities,facilities, timing, atmosphere.. etc

Every time he asked me how my session was.My response was negative majorly. I said "these things should be changed"

He changed my opinion by his saying "to change you need to accept situation first, enter in atmosphere and then bring the changes you want, to change the inner world you need to go in first"That was the end of my complaining habit.

Lesson:

•You cannot change inside by standing outside

•Complaining makes you ungrateful.

•Use the availabilities to change

•Positive thinking brings positive change

ADVISE PRIVATELY

I was around 10 years old when I was loved

by everyone because of my talkative nature

but I usually used to mistreat my elders. Once

it so happened that I disrespected one of our

elder, when my father(abbu) got to know

about this matter he called me in his room

and asked me to narrate the whole matter

I did accordingly and he asked me "do you

think what you said was right?" I answered

negatively and he replied "correct your mistake

by apologizing" and I apologized.

I was angry at that moment but now I understood

why he made me to apologise.

Lesson:

•Advising privately is most effective way of correcting.

•Do not humiliate while advising.

•Correct your advising way before correcting others

•Correcting someone's mistake openly is a biggest

mistake

PRAY FOR REPENTANCE

I created a social account which I used to have fun or chat with opposite gender, my dad used to observe me every now and then that I was busy in phone but never questioned me and I thought I had freedom to do whatever I want with my account, but my dad knew what i was upto.

One day he asked me to read Qur'an (religious book) which quoted "my son, indeed if wrong should be the weight of a mustard seed and should be within a rock or [anywhere] in the heavens or in the earth, Allah will bring it forth"(31:16).

He turned towards me saying"you think we don't know but Allah knows it" I cried before him because I knew I was committing a sin but I didn't wanted to leave it because I was enjoying.

Lesson:

•If it's a sin then it is, even if whole world is doing it

 •Purely Qur'an is a book for guidance

•Do not go back to sin once you have been guided.

•Loving or knowingly committing a sin is a major sin

•beware of sins as most are easily approachable on social media

•beware of sins as most are easily approachable on social media

STRICT FOR RELIGION

I was around 12/13 years old, I participated in running race and the competition was in the month of Ramadan and I was fasting even after knowing about the race my dad allowed me to fast. I reached the school all of my friends forced me to break the fast and thus just before lunch time I broke the fast, I went back home for lunch and not to get scolded I took along my cousin sister to home who wasn't fasting, I went near mother and informed about it all she said was "go near your father" and I went near him and he said "how dare that you even entered this house after breaking the fast" I was feared and after an hour of crying I had lunch though I won the race but failed in my fasting.

Lesson:

•Religion comes first no matter what

•You will be serious if you find your elders serious about it.

•Real race is the race of good deeds collection for the last day.

•You can't escape after committing a sin

•fear of Allah should be greater than fear of parents

TREAT YOUR MOTHER RIGHT

One day it happened that my mother and my elder sister had an argument, it turned worst when my mother cried because of behaviour of my sister and my mother didn't spoke to any one after the argument, till my father reached home and when he got to know the matter he called all of us(4 daughters)he said "your mother hasn't raised you all for this day she has already enough body pain and I don't expect emotional pain from you all what happened today should not be repeated as what was lost today was not the tears of mother but your level of Jannah" as we stood in front of him hearing, and we could feel his voice changing from hard to soft because of the pain his wife felt because of children.

Lesson:

•Act strict when you need to.

•Have a balance in the family for righteous atmosphere

•Being a parent make your kids to respect your spouse

•kids will learn by seeing how you treat others

•The biggest loss is the loss of a mother's tear because of

your ill treatment

WARN BEFORE ACTION

I was selected for interschool competition during school days and at last minute I got to know that in a form one needs their respective parents signature, and needed to be submitted on that day itself and on my teacher's advise, I copied my father's signature on it and after reaching home I admitted my mistake to my father he got angry but later permitted me to go out of school to play but while returning it was dark and we returned all the way standing as we couldn't sit this irked my father and he complained about the maintainance and later made me realise that because of that one signature I had to face this situation.

Lesson:

•Admit your mistake before it's too late

•Even after realising you need to bear the consequences of your mistake.

•Do not commit mistake because of other's pressure.

Let your kid learn on his own from his mistakes

GUIDE BUT DON'T FORCE

As I said earlier, I loved to teach about religion and I remember how excited I was for my first ever lecture a day before my dad asked me to illustrate my preparation he helped me to add some more points and then next day I made a video he heard every line twice and advised me about how can I improve my teaching skills, he stills calls me to advise whenever he hears that am going to a new place he says all about the place, people and how should I be conscious while giving dawah. Though i knew my talent but he was the one who nourished it and brought my talent out beautifully .And my mom used to travel with me for lectures just to guide me. Alhamdulillah

Lesson:

•Do not interrupt when Let your kid is trying something new Only way of helping your kid is to Advise him

•Do not force your kid let him hunt his talent on his own

•Guide your kid gracefully

Forcing your kid to be what you want is like killing of his talent

BE AWARE OF WHAT YOU SAY

I attended a religious lecture and was waiting to return to home , and there I saw some funny news which I extended to make others laugh by adding words which were not true, my elder sister who was also with me noticed this and informed my mother. my mother inquired about this to me and I found myself guilty about my behavior and she warned me by making me realise how Grievous this sin was where I could miss a house of Paradise. What I learnt was.

Lesson

•Do not say which isn't true.

•Do not add words to make others laugh

•Excessive talking is a poison of heart

•Think twice before you speak

SPEND TIME WITH YOURSELF

I had some free time before my semester classes, my dad sent me to a workshop paying around thousands of rupees even he was a participant there, the place of workshop was beyond amazing with birds, plants, fishes, pool,..etc. various people from various places I didn't even knew how speed these 10 days went. Initially I didn't wanted to join but I joined only because my father wanted to. He knew what was best for me and in those 10 days I nourished myself, found the real me, made some new and senior friends and I am a certified councillor now but the most amazing thing I felt was a feeling that my dad is a human, with feelings because he cried infront of all participants while sharing his journey and I realised that my Father is an amazing human with emotions.

Lesson:

Let your kid spend some time alone

*Allow your kid to meet himself

Help your kid to reach new levels of his talent

•Let your family travel be worthy enough to be remembered

•Keep an eye on your kid but do not spy on them

TAKE OPINIONS SERIOUSLY

I was reading in room when all of a sudden my dad entered

and asked me about further studies I said I would not like

to continue it as am not interested he then asked me about

marriage proposal he recieved, I just Heard him silently

and then he asked me what type of spouse do I dream of?

this was the question I never expected yet I replied that I

was quite clear of a spouse who has a quality of helping

me in dawah that's it...he then heard me patiently and

while accepting the proposal he said the same words that

my work towards my religion should not stop. At my

school friends get together I was asked did my

father asked me about quality of husband? I replied positively saying "yes I am going to marry with man who I want and with

qualities I admired of" they replied "lucky enough that

your guardian atleast asks you because her marriage

was fixed without asking her in detail"

Lesson:

•Let your kid decide about their future

•Know your kid's idea first then give opinion

Forcing your decision on them is like murdering their desires

Show them that it is their life and they are important as well

Take their opinions seriously and listen to your kids

THE LAST ADVISE

Finally I was married and before I could leave with my husband to his House, my eyes were constantly searching for my dad longing to see him one more time, I waited for him for a while and finally he came, towards me with a smile and tearful eyes holding my hand, taking me from stage to the car he said few words which are imprinted in my mind, he said

"Dear daughter, do not pressurise your mind with questions like why/how/when/what, however the house is do not expect anything, However things are going let them go do not overthink about it"

This is the first stage of marriage (physical relation) everything seems beautiful and wonderful,

the second one(understanding) everyone, every relation,

family with time this stage settles you.

the third stage (sacrifice one) do not complain while doing
so,

fourth stage(helping one) you will be old while reaching

that all matters will be memories you made in earlier

two stages

but one thing should not stop among all these stages

is love because this is the backbone of all stages

LOVE IS TO CARE

When me and my mom were alone when my little sister climbed on kitchen's roof for craft work but she slipped and hit her eye so hard that she started bleeding, the sound was so hard we rushed to see her lying on her back and we took her to hospital and she was fine but her eyes turned blue.my mom scolded her till she came back from hospital but when she came to knew that she fell from top she started crying"o my daughter, what have you done to yourself.." I was staring at her instant changed reaction .I prayed for her that she was safe enough but this incident had a deep impact

What I learnt was....

Lesson

•there is no limit for mother's love

•Love can be expressed in many ways

•Love is to take care of your loved ones

•You realise one's love when they are hurt

TRUE WELL WISHERS

I realised the value of my parents only when I left the house after getting married, though there was same day and night but a single day without them was like a year.

Every day waking up to find that now you have to be responsible was not difficult but the people who used to care for you help you and lead you in life were not with you was the difficult thing to accept and to continue life without them.

Parents are the only well wishers in your life who always expect and give you the best

ABOUT PARENTS

Let's see what Qur'an says about the parents

Quranic verse-1

And We have enjoined upon man, to his parents, good treatment. His mother carried him with hardship and gave birth to him with hardship, and his gestation and weaning [period] is thirty months. [He grows] until, when he reaches maturity(46:15)

Quranic verse-2

"and to parents do good and to relatives"(2:83)

Quranic verse-4

"Our Lord, forgive me and my parents and the believers the Day the account is established"(14:41)

Quranic verse-3

"My Lord, enable me to be grateful for Your favor which You have bestowed upon me and upon my parents and to do righteousness of which You approve"(27:19)

Quranic verse-5

"But one who says to his parents, "Uff to you; do you promise me that I will be brought forth [from the earth] when generations before me have already passed on [into oblivion]?" while they call to Allah for help [and to their son], "Woe to you! Believe! Indeed, the promise of Allah is truth."(46:17)

Quranic verse-6

"My Lord, forgive me and my parents and whoever enters my house a believer and the believing men and believing women." (71:28)

RIGHTS OF PARENTS

Right to be respected

Right to be obeyed

Right to hear kind words

Right to be behaved good

Right to be reprimand and rebuke

Right to be helped

Right to be looked after.

RIGHTS OF CHILDREN

Right to provision

Right to protection

Right to love

Right to affection

Right to paternity

Right to inheritance

Right of proper education

Appendix

Let this page be for my husband, shahebaz Ahmed

Well I am newly married and I have a 6 month old son, everything changed after the birth of our son.

I couldn't even feel the love around me Because I thought everything was around the newborn.

A New phase of life brought new challenges to both of us

But Alhamdulillah,

He actively took part in my changes , loved me more so that I should not feel alone or stuck, sometimes helps me with household chores , takes special care of child and keeps our childish behaviour alive.

Words fall short to describe how wonderful this journey have been with him in sha allah there will be yet more to come as I love to try new things when he is there beside me

Thankyou for helping me to adjust the household chores and child . Most importantly thank you for letting me enjoy my own me time where I can spend freely the time with myself and books

Thank you for being the shoulder where I relieve my emotional stress and thank you for carrying out our responsibility on your strong shoulder.

Thankyou for being the blessing Alhamdulillah.

Glossary

You can also follow me

On Instagram where I share islamic posts

@nabi_e_ummah

@charge_ur_eemaan

You can also mail me

www.firdosetarannum@gmail.com

List of Contributors

I would like to dedicate my words to

My lord first who gave me enough strength and knowledge to put my love in beautiful form

My father : MA maruf(my inspiration)

My mother: shahenaz khanam (my blessing)

My sisters: sadiya sarshar(I admire her)

Fariha mubasshera(the perfect one).

Zuha Battul(my favourite one)

My brother: Hamdan Zaki(loved for being one)

My spouse: Shahebaz Ahmed (my biggest supporter)

Notes

Here I would like to say something about myself

Well , I am firdos Tarannum

At a very young age I experienced many of life opportunities like teaching experience while I was a student, attending workshop and councilling people ..etc

Although now am married to shahebaz Ahmed who is responsible for inspiring me to write and read and continue my hobby which is slowly turning into a passion handling home with a 6 month old kid seems tiring but he was supportive that he always helped me with baby , household chores and especially my love towards my reading.

My aim is to be a motivational speaker, to be a councillor so that I can help people with mental health problems and a lecturer but I never thought that Allah would bless me with a child so soon and whenever I look at him it feels like I need to work or read so that he continues the legacy of reading like am doing so by watching my dad who loves reading.